CONTENTS

CHAPTER 1

A TALE FROM PRISON

In the late 1200s, the European cities of Genoa and Venice were at war. They were fighting to control trade in the Mediterranean Sea.

By 1298, war prisoners filled Genoa's jail. Among them was a Venetian trader with an unbelievable tale. Prisoners gathered in the jail's large common room to listen to his story.

Did Marco Polo really see man-eating snakes in China?

Shhh! He's about to begin.

At the time, Europeans knew little about China. The prisoners thought it was a strange land filled with odd creatures and great riches.

In 1271, Marco's wish came true.

Niccoló and Maffeo had promised Kublai Khan, the ruler of the vast Mongol Empire, that they would return to China. Kublai Khan wanted them to bring him news from the pope, the leader of the Roman Catholic Church.

Father, what are you looking for?

We have to be watchful. There may be pirates in these waters.

The Polos' ship landed in the city of Ayas, in what is now Turkey. Then they travelled along the Silk Road, which was a series of trade routes that connected Asia and Europe.

. . . and the vast Gobi Desert.

It took the Polos a month to cross the Gobi Desert. The nights were cold, and the days were hot. People said that evil spirits roamed the desert.

Uncle, someone's calling my name.

Don't listen, Marco.

You'll become lost forever if you follow the spirits into the desert.

Niccoló and Maffeo presented Kublai Khan with gifts, such as crystal vases and oil from a holy place in Jerusalem. This oil was said to have healing powers. They also delivered a letter from Pope Gregory X.

I thank you for these precious gifts, but . . .

Something interested Kublai Khan more than the gifts.

You must tell me all that you see and learn.

The Mongol empire was very large. Kublai Khan could not visit every part of his kingdom. He hoped to learn more about the lands he ruled through Marco's travels.

Have a safe journey, son.

CHAPTER 3

EXPLORING AN EMPIRE

While in the service of Kublai Khan, Marco went on several trips. He visited the kingdom's large cities. Marco was amazed by the goods being traded in the city marketplaces.

The cloth is made of gold and silk.

Marco travelled to different parts of Kublai Khan's vast empire.

What is this province called?

It is known as Tibet.

In his travels, Marco met all kinds of people. In southern Asia, he visited a group of people who covered their bodies with tattoos.

Their flesh is covered all over with pictures of lions and dragons and birds.

While telling his story to the prisoners, Marco described animals that most Europeans had never seen. So he compared them to animals that were familiar to Europeans. He spoke of crocodiles as large snakes.

In one province live huge serpents . . . some of them are more than 20 feet long . . . Their mouths are big enough to swallow a man in one gulp. Their teeth are huge.

Marco said tigers were striped lions.

There are lions of immense size, bigger than those of Egypt. They have beautiful fur, with stripes of black, orange, and white.

Marco even said he saw unicorns. What he really described were rhinoceroses.

They have plenty of unicorns, which are scarcely smaller than elephants. They have the hair of a buffalo and feet like an elephant's. They have a single large, black horn in the middle of the forehead.

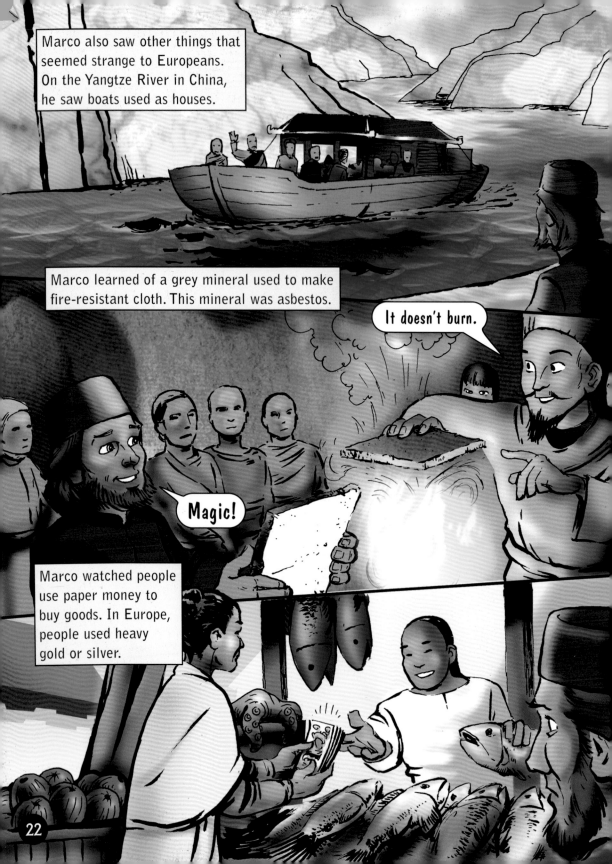

Marco also saw other things that seemed strange to Europeans. On the Yangtze River in China, he saw boats used as houses.

Marco learned of a grey mineral used to make fire-resistant cloth. This mineral was asbestos.

It doesn't burn.

Magic!

Marco watched people use paper money to buy goods. In Europe, people used heavy gold or silver.

CHAPTER 4

THE GRAND STORYTELLER

After serving the Great Khan for 17 years, my father, uncle, and I decided it was time to return home. But Kublai Khan had one last task for us. He wanted us to take his niece, Princess Kokachin, to Persia.

In 1292, we left with 14 ships. . . .

The Polos had a horrible sea voyage. Storms sank many of the ships. Sailors died of sickness. The Polos arrived safely with the princess, but only one ship survived the 18-month journey.

Marco's story will make a great book.

The book about Marco's adventure became known as *The Travels of Marco Polo*. It was very popular in Europe.

Over the next 200 years, Europeans did not travel to the parts of Asia that Marco described. Many Asian rulers closed their land borders to foreigners. But Marco's stories inspired other explorers, such as ChristopherColumbus. Explorers hoped to discover a sea route that could be used to carry trade goods from Asia back to Europe. This was eventually achieved in the late 1400s by Portuguese explorer Vasco da Gama.

More about Marco Polo

- ➤ Marco Polo was born in 1254 on the island of Korcula. This island was ruled by the city of Venice at the time. It is now part of Croatia.

- ➤ Marco's mother died while Niccoló and Maffeo were on their first trip to China. Marco was raised by his aunt.

- ➤ Marco did not really hear evil spirits while travelling through the Gobi Desert. The sounds people heard were created by the wind blowing through plants and trees.

- ➤ Genoa and Venice fought four wars to gain control of trade routes in the Mediterranean Sea. Marco fought in the second war, which lasted from 1293 to 1299.

- ➤ Marco was taken prisoner on 6 September 1298, in a sea battle near the island of Korcula. The Venetians lost almost all of their ships, and about 14,000 sailors were either killed or captured during the battle.

- ➤ Marco was released from prison in 1299. He died in 1324 in Venice.

➤ Kublai Khan asked the Polos to bring him 100 religious men who could teach him about Christianity. Only two such men agreed to join the Polos. But they quickly grew afraid during the long, dangerous journey to China and returned home.

➤ Kublai Khan was the grandson of the great Mongol leader Genghis Khan. The Mongol Empire created by Genghis Khan was the largest land empire in history. At one time, the Mongols ruled nearly all the land from Korea and China to eastern Europe.

➤ Many historians do not believe that Marco Polo ever went to China. They point out that Marco did not mention the Great Wall of China, an important landmark. Historians say that what is really important is the way in which *The Travels of Marco Polo* affected people in Europe. Marco's book inspired people to learn more about China and to find a sea route to Asia. In searching for a sea route, explorers learned about parts of the world that were previously uknown.

GLOSSARY

ambassador person who represents a government in another country

asbestos greyish mineral whose fibers can be woven into fireproof fabric

caravan group of people travelling together

custom tradition among a group of people

province district or region of some countries

tattoo picture that has been printed on to someone's skin with needles and ink

INTERNET SITES

http://www.bbc.co.uk/history/historic_figures/polo_marco.shtml
Visit this website for a brief history of the life and death of Marco Polo.

www.funtrivia.com/flashquiz/index.cfm?qid=71596
Visit this website and test your knowledge with a fun quiz about Marco Polo. What will you score?

READ MORE

Ancient China (Early Civilizations), Kathleen W. Deady and Muriel L. Dubois (Capstone Press, 2003)

Marco Polo: From Venice to the Far East, Clint Twist (Templar, 2010)

Marco Polo and the Realm of Kublai Khan (Explorers of New Lands), Tim McNeese (Chelsea House, 2005)

Marco Polo: Overland to China (In the Footsteps of Explorers), Alexander Zelenyi (Crabtree, 2010)

BIBLIOGRAPHY

Did Marco Polo Go to China?, Frances Wood (Secker & Warburg, 1995)

Khubilai Khan: His Life and Times, Morris Rossabi (University of California Press, 1988)

The Marco Polo Expedition: A Journey along the Silk Road, Richard B. Fisher (Hodder and Stoughton, 1988)

The Travels of Marco Polo, Marco Polo, Translated by Ronald Latham (Penguin Books, 1988)

INDEX